Piano • Vocal • Guitar

D0613746

ISBN-13: 978-1-4234-3139-8
ISBN-10: 1-4234-3139-1

7777 W. Bluemound Rd. P.O. Box 13819 Milwaukee, WI 53213

In Australia Contact:
Hal Leonard Australia Pty. Ltd.
4 Lentara Court
Cheltenham, Victoria, 3192 Australia
Email: ausadmin@halleonard.com

For all works contained herein:
Unauthorized copying, arranging, adapting, recording or public performance is an infringement of copyright.
Infringers are liable under the law.

Visit Hal Leonard Online at
www.halleonard.com

4 Girlfriend

13 I C@n Do Better

21 Run@w@y

29 The Be$t D@mn Thing

37 When You're Gone

43 Everything B@ck But You

52 Hot

60 Innocence

69 I Don't H@ve to Try

77 One of Tho$e Girl$

85 Cont@gious

90 Keep Holding On

GIRLFRIEND

Words and Music by AVRIL LAVIGNE
and LUKASZ GOTTWALD

Moderately fast Rock

N.C.

Hey, hey, you, you, I don't like your girl - friend. No way, no way, I
Hey, hey, you, you, I know that you like me. No way, no way, _

mf

think you need a new one. Hey, hey, you, you, I could be your girl - friend.
no, it's not a se - cret. Hey, hey, you, you, I want to be your girl - friend.

D5 (5fr) F♯5 G5 (3fr) N.C.

You're so fine, I want you

Copyright © 2007 ALMO MUSIC CORP., AVRIL LAVIGNE PUBLISHING LTD., KOBALT SONGS MUSIC PUBLISHING and KASZ MONEY PUBLISHING
All Rights for AVRIL LAVIGNE PUBLISHING LTD. Controlled and Administered by ALMO MUSIC CORP.
All Rights for KASZ MONEY PUBLISHING Controlled and Administered by KOBALT SONGS MUSIC PUBLISHING
All Rights Reserved Used by Permission

A5
5fr
mine, you're so de - li - cious. I think a - bout you all the time, you're so ad - dic - tive.
B5
G5
3fr
Don't you know what I could do to make you feel al - right, al - right, al - right,
D5
5fr
al - right, al - right? Don't pre - tend, I think you know I'm damn pre - cious.
A5
5fr
B5
And hell yeah, I'm the moth - er - **** - in' prin - cess. I can tell you like me

G5
3fr
too and you know I'm right, I'm right, I'm right, I'm right, I'm right.
B5
F♯sus
She's like so what - ev - er. You could do
Asus2
so much bet - ter. I think we should get to - geth - er now
G5
3fr
A5
5fr
D5
5fr
A5
5fr
and that's what ev - 'ry - one's talk - in' a - bout. Hey, hey, you, you,

B5 G5 D5 A5 B5 G5
I don't like your girl - friend. No way, no way, I think you need a new one.
D5 A5 B5 G5 D5 F♯5
Hey, hey, you, you, I could be your girl - friend.
G5 D5 A5 B5 G5
Hey, hey, you, you, I know that you like me.
D5 A5 B5 G5 D5 A5
No way, no way, no, it's not a se - cret. Hey, hey, you, you, I

B5
G5
3fr
D5
5fr
F♯5
G5
3fr
To Coda
want to be your girl - friend.
N.C.
A5
5fr
I can see the way, I see the way you look at me.
And e - ven when you look a -
B5
way, I know you think of me.
I know you talk a - bout me all the time a - gain and a - gain.
G5
3fr
D5
5fr
So come, so come o - ver here and

A5
5fr
tell me what I want to hear.
Bet - ter yet, make your girl - friend dis - ap - pear.
B5
G5
3fr
I don't wan - na hear you say her name ev - er a - gain, and a - gain, and a - gain,
D.S. al Coda
and a - gain. 'Cause.
CODA
D5
5fr
N.C.
Uhh, in a sec - ond you'll be wrapped a - round my fin - ger
'cause I can, 'cause I can do it bet - ter.
There's no oth - er, so

when's it gon - na sink in? She's so stu - pid, what the hell were you think - in'?
Hey, hey, you, you, I don't like your girl - friend. No way, no way, I
think you need a new one. Hey, hey, you, you, I could be your girl - friend.
D5
5fr
F♯5
G5
3fr
D5
5fr
A5
5fr
No way, no way.
Hey, hey, you, you,

B5 G5 D5 A5 B5 G5
I know that you like me. No way, no way, no, it's not a se - cret.
D5 A5 B5 G5 D5 F♯5
Hey, hey, you, you, I want to be your girl - friend. No way, no
G5 D5 A5 B5 G5
way, hey. Hey, hey, you, you, I don't like your girl - friend.
D5 A5 B5 G5 D5 A5
No way, no way, I think you need a new one. Hey, hey, you, you,

B5 G5 D5 F♯5 G5
I could be your girl - friend.
No way, no way, hey.
D5 A5 B5 G5 D5 A5
Hey, hey, you, you, I know that you like me. No way, no way,
B5 G5 D5 A5 B5 G5
no, it's not a se - cret. Hey, hey, you, you, I want to be your girl - friend.
No
D5 F♯5 G5 D5
way, no way, hey, hey.

I CAN DO BETTER

Words and Music by AVRIL LAVIGNE
and LUKASZ GOTTWALD

Copyright © 2007 ALMO MUSIC CORP., AVRIL LAVIGNE PUBLISHING LTD., KOBALT SONGS MUSIC PUBLISHING and KASZ MONEY PUBLISHING
All Rights for AVRIL LAVIGNE PUBLISHING LTD. Controlled and Administered by ALMO MUSIC CORP.
All Rights for KASZ MONEY PUBLISHING Controlled and Administered by KOBALT SONGS MUSIC PUBLISHING
All Rights Reserved Used by Permission

F5
C5
3fr
what you think of me, 'cause ei - ther way, you're gon - na
just can't com - pre - hend. I don't think that you
G5
3fr
think what you be - lieve. There's noth - ing you could say
can han - dle it. I'm way o - ver,
F5
C5
3fr
that would hurt me. I'm bet - ter off with - out
o - ver it. I will drink as much
G5
3fr
you an - y - way. I thought it would be hard,
Li - mon - cel - lo as I can, and I'll do it a - gain

F5
C5
3fr
but I'm o - kay. I don't need you if you're
and a - gain. I don't real - ly care
G5
3fr
gon - na be that way, 'cause with me it's
what you have to say, 'cause you know, you
F5
A5
5fr
all or noth - ing.
know you're noth - ing.
I'm sick of this / your shit, don't de - ny
F5
A5
5fr
you're a waste of time. I'm sick of this / your

F5
G5
3fr
shit, don't ask why. I hate
C
G7(no3)
you now, so go a - way
Am
from me. You're gone, so long; I
Fsus2
can do bet - ter, I can do bet - ter. Hey,

C
hey you,
I found
G7(no3)
my - self
a - gain.
That's why
Am
you're gone.
I
Fsus2
can do bet - ter, I
can do bet - ter.

N.C.
What'd ya say?
I'm ___ so
I told you so.
sick of you.
You know that,
You're on my nerves.
'cause I al - ways know.
I want to puke.
Get out of my face,
hey, hey.
You're not my taste,
hey, hey.
Hey, hey,
Hey, hey.
I hate ___

C
G7(no3)
you now, so go a - way
Am
from me. You're gone, so long;
Fsus2
I can do bet - ter, I
C
can do bet - ter. Hey, hey you,

G7(no3)
I found my - self
Am
a - gain. That's why you're gone.
Fsus2
I can do bet - ter, I
1
can do bet - ter. I hate
2
can do bet - ter.
C5
3fr

RUNAWAY

Words and Music by AVRIL LAVIGNE,
LUKASZ GOTTWALD and KARA DioGUARDI

Copyright © 2007 ALMO MUSIC CORP., AVRIL LAVIGNE PUBLISHING LTD., KOBALT SONGS MUSIC PUBLISHING, KASZ MONEY PUBLISHING and K'STUFF PUBLISHING
All Rights for AVRIL LAVIGNE PUBLISHING LTD. Controlled and Administered by ALMO MUSIC CORP.
All Rights for KASZ MONEY PUBLISHING Controlled and Administered by KOBALT SONGS MUSIC PUBLISHING
All Rights Reserved Used by Permission

C5
G5
F
G5
3fr
like it's just one of those kind of days. You
can't kick me down; I'm al - read - y on the ground. No, you
so is how I'm do - ing, if you're won - der - ing. I'm in a
can't but you could - n't catch me an - y - how. Blue
fight with the world but I'm win - ning. Stay
skies, but the sun is - n't com - ing out, no. To -
there, come clos - er; it's at your own risk. Yeah, you

C5 G5 F G5 C G5 F5
3fr
day it's like I'm un - der a heav - y cloud.
know how it is; life can be a bitch.
And I
G5 C G5 F5 G5
feel so a - live.
I can't help my - self,
C G5 F5 G5 C G5 F5
don't you re - al - ize.
G5 Am C5
I just wan - na scream and lose con - trol,

C/F
3fr
throw my hands up and let it go, for -
Am
C5
3fr
C/F
3fr
get a - bout ev - 'ry - thing and run a - way,
yeah.
Am
I just want to fall and lose
C5
3fr
my - self,
C/F
3fr
laugh - ing so hard it hurts

Am
like hell, for - get a - bout ev - 'ry - thing
C5
3fr
C/F
3fr
1
and run a - way, yeah.
C5
3fr
G5
3fr
F5
G5
3fr
2
So - yeah.
Am7
C5
3fr
C/F
3fr
Run a - way, run a - way.

Am7
C5
3fr
Run a - way, run a - way.
C/F
3fr
Am9
5fr
Run a - way, run
C5
3fr
C/F
3fr
a - way.
Run a - way, run, run a - way.
Am9
5fr
C5
3fr
C/F
3fr
Run a - way, run a - way.
Run a - way, run,

Am
run a - way.
I just wan - na scream and lose
C5
3fr
C/F
3fr
con - trol,
throw my hands up and let
Am
it go,
for - get a - bout ev - 'ry - thing
C5
3fr
C/F
3fr
and run a - way,
yeah.

Am
C5
3fr
I just want to fall and lose my - self,
C/F
3fr
laugh - ing so hard it hurts like hell, for -
Am
C5
3fr
get a - bout ev - 'ry - thing and run a -
C/F
3fr
way, yeah.
Am

THE BEST DAMN THING

Words and Music by AVRIL LAVIGNE
and BUTCH WALKER

Copyright © 2007 ALMO MUSIC CORP., AVRIL LAVIGNE PUBLISHING LTD., EMI BLACKWOOD MUSIC INC. and SONOTROCK MUSIC
All Rights for AVRIL LAVIGNE PUBLISHING LTD. Controlled and Administered by ALMO MUSIC CORP.
All Rights for SONOTROCK MUSIC Controlled and Administered by EMI BLACKWOOD MUSIC INC.
All Rights Reserved Used by Permission

though I told him yes - ter - day and the day be - fore. I
cer - tain time of month I don't wan - na hold his hand. I
hate it when a guy does - n't get the tab and I
hate it when they go out and we stay in, and they
G5
3fr
have to put my mon - ey out, and that looks bad.
come home smell - ing like their ex - girl - friend.
Bm9
Gmaj9
(1., 3.) Where are the hopes, where are the dreams,
(2.) But I found my hopes, I found my dreams,

D
A/C♯
my Cin - der - el - la sto - ry scene?
my Cin - der - el - la sto - ry scene.
Bm
G
A
When do you think they'll fin - 'ly see
Now ev - 'ry - bod - y's gon - na see
D5
5fr
that you're not, not, not gon - na get
that you're not, not, not gon - na get
D/G
an - y bet - ter?
an - y bet - ter.
You won't, won't, won't, you won't get

Bm7
rid of me, nev - er. Like it or not, e - ven though
Asus
D/G
she's a lot like me, we're not the same.
D/F♯
G5
3fr
D5
5fr
And yeah, yeah, yeah, I'm a lot
D/G
to han - dle. You don't know trou - ble; I'm a

Bm7
hell of a scan - dal. Me, I'm a scene, I'm a
G5
3fr
To Coda
dra - ma queen, I'm the best damn thing that your
1
A5
5fr
D5
5fr
eyes have ev - er seen. Al - right,
al - right, yeah. I

2
A5
5fr
A5
5fr
Give me an A.
eyes have ev - er seen.
(Al - ways
give me what I want.) Give me a V.
(Be ver - y,
ver - y good to me.
R.
(Are you gon - na treat me right?)
I.
(I can put up a fight.) Give me an

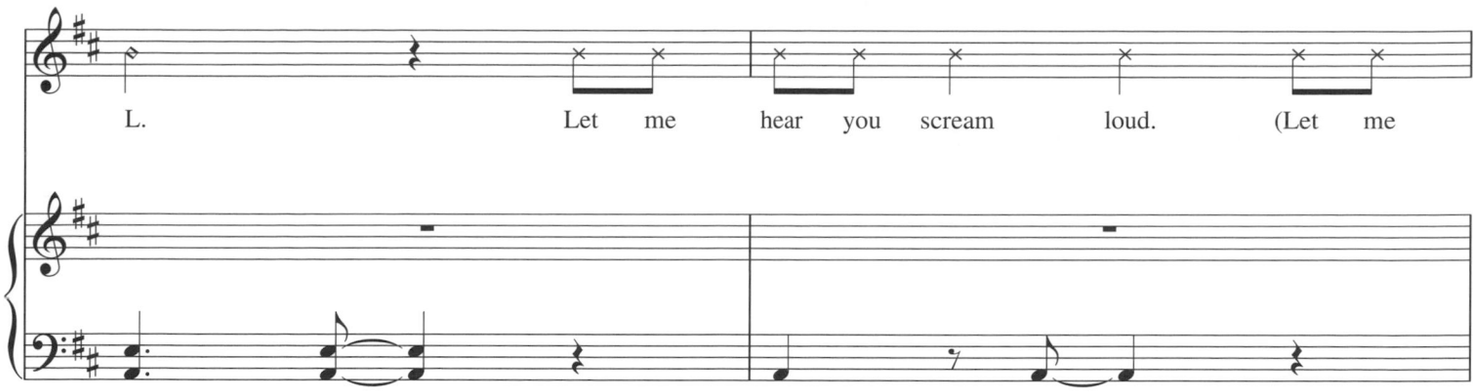
L. Let me hear you scream loud. (Let me

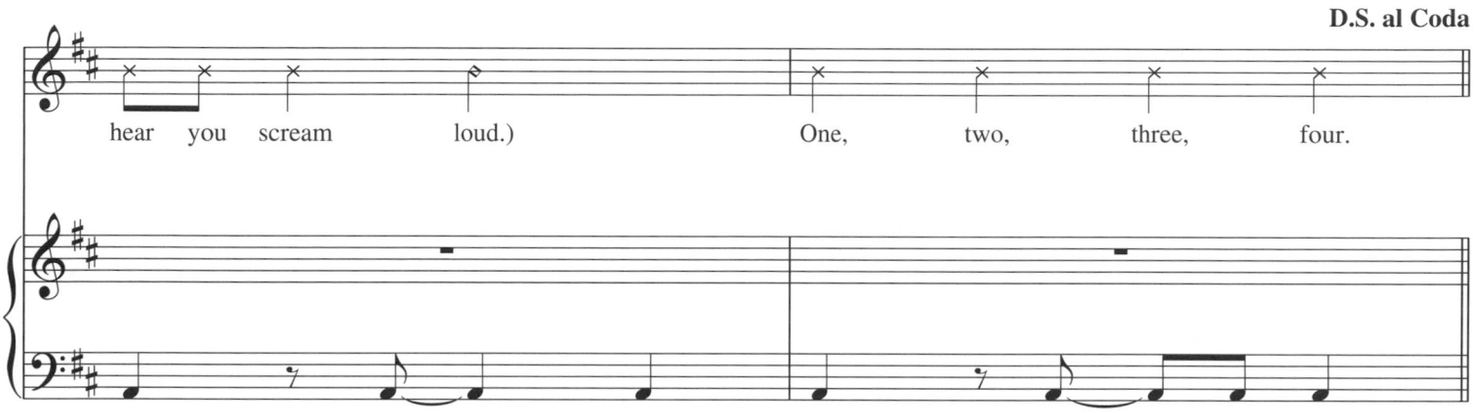
D.S. al Coda
hear you scream loud.) One, two, three, four.

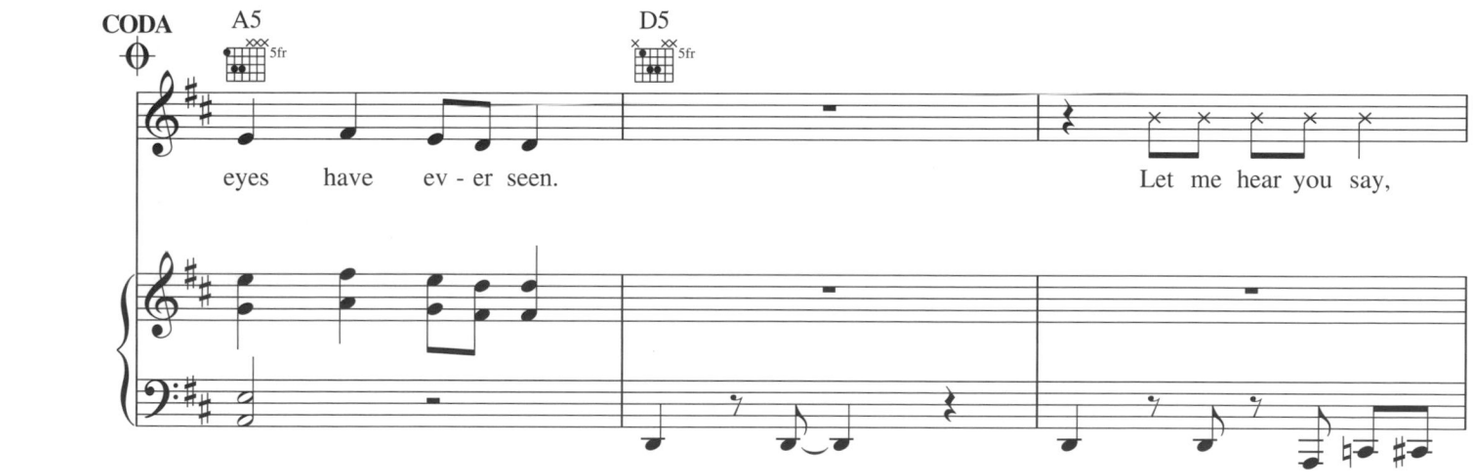
CODA
A5
5fr
D5
5fr
eyes have ev - er seen.
Let me hear you say,

"Hey, hey, hey!"
(Hey, hey, hey!)
Al - right,

now let me hear you say, "Hey, hey, ho!" (Hey, hey, ho!)
D5
5fr
(Hey, hey, hey!)
(Hey, hey, hey!)
(Hey, hey, hey!) I'm the
G5
3fr
A5
5fr
D5
5fr
best damn thing that your eyes have ev - er seen.

WHEN YOU'RE GONE

Words and Music by AVRIL LAVIGNE
and BUTCH WALKER

Copyright © 2007 ALMO MUSIC CORP., AVRIL LAVIGNE PUBLISHING LTD., EMI BLACKWOOD MUSIC INC. and SONOTROCK MUSIC
All Rights for AVRIL LAVIGNE PUBLISHING LTD. Controlled and Administered by ALMO MUSIC CORP.
All Rights for SONOTROCK MUSIC Controlled and Administered by EMI BLACKWOOD MUSIC INC.
All Rights Reserved Used by Permission

G
D/F♯
Em7
days feel like years when I'm a - lone, and the bed where you lie
clothes you left, they lie on the floor, and they smell just like you.
C
D
Dsus2
D
is made up on your side.
I love the things that you do.
When
Am7
G/B
you walk a - way, I count the steps that you take. Do you
Cmaj9♯11
D5
5fr
see how much I need you right now? When you're gone,

Cmaj9
Em7
D
the piec - es of my heart are miss-ing you. When you're gone,
Cmaj9
Em7
D
the face I came to know is miss-ing too. When you're gone,
Am7
C(add2)
G
D/F♯
the words I need to hear to al - ways get me through the day
C(add2)
1
D
and make it O - K... I miss you.

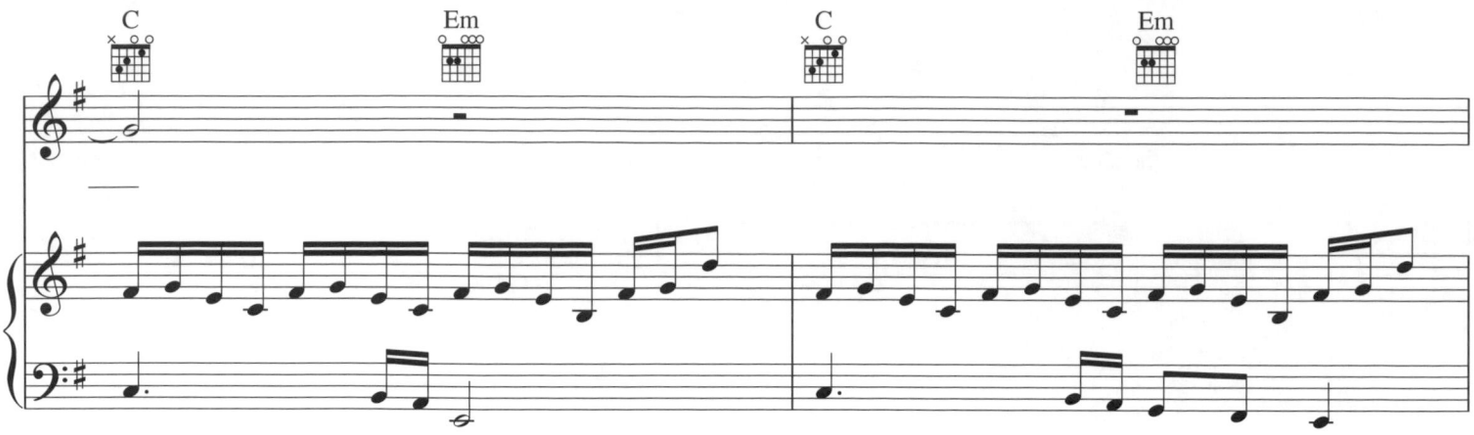
C
Em
C
Em

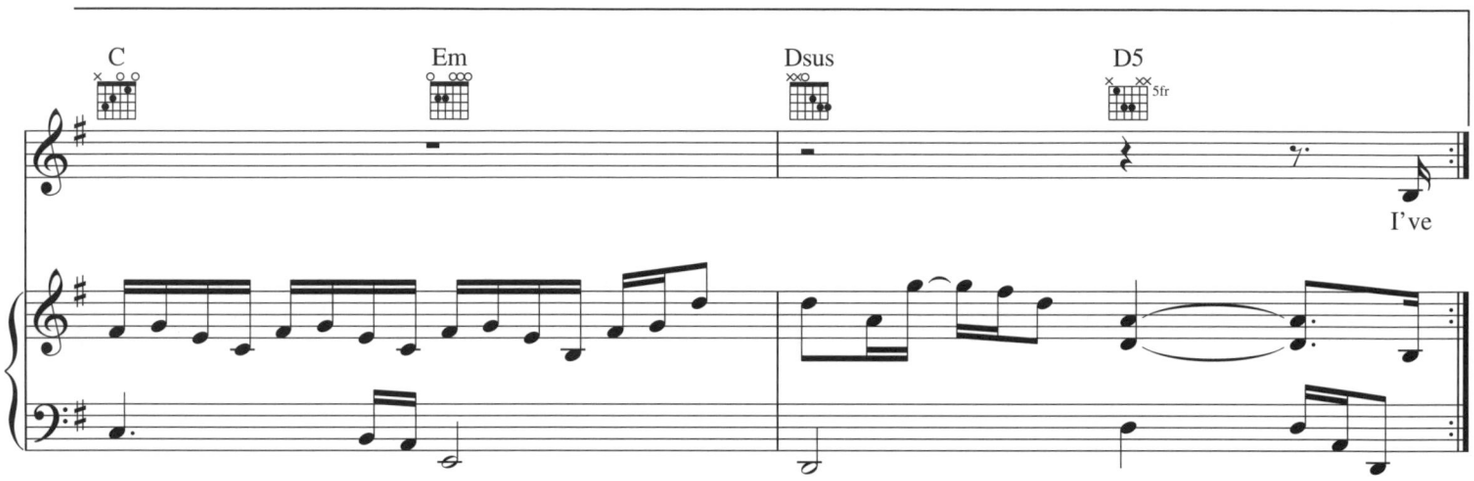
C
Em
Dsus
D5
5fr
I've

2
D(add4)
3fr
Bm
I miss you.
We were made for each oth -

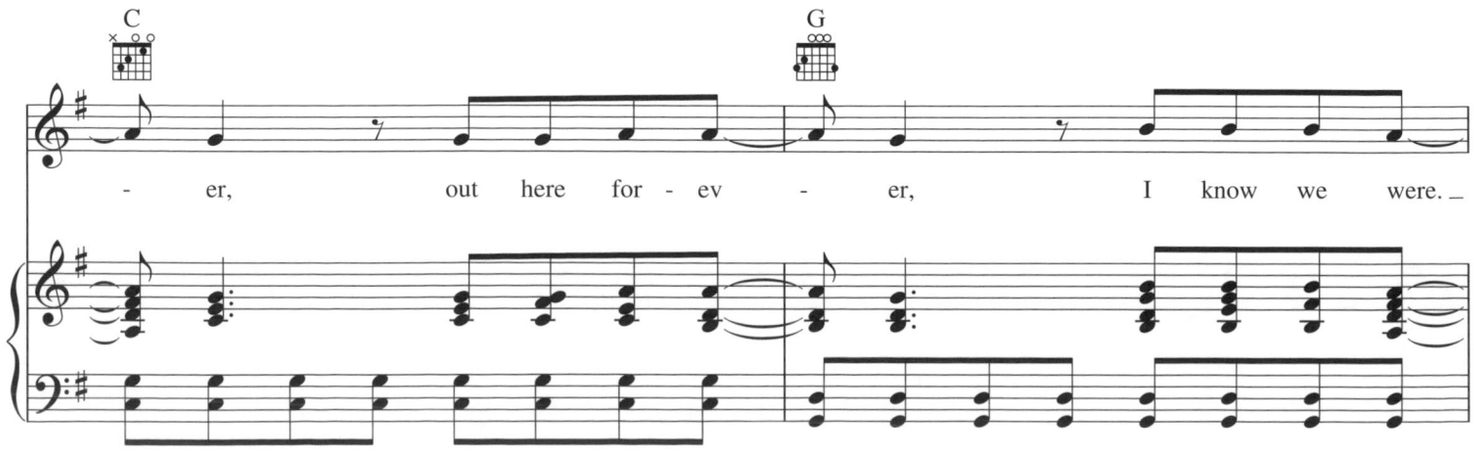
C
G
- er, out here for - ev - er, I know we were.

D
B7
Em
Esus
Em
Yeah, yeah.
All I ev - er want-ed was for you to know,
C
D/C
Cmaj7
C♯m7♭5
4fr
ev-'ry-thing I do, I give my heart and soul.
I can hard-ly breathe; I need to feel you here with me.
D
Cmaj9
Em7
When you're gone,
the piec - es of my heart
D
Cmaj9
Em7
are miss-ing you.
When you're gone,
the face I came to know

D
Am7
C(add2)
is miss-ing too. When you're gone, the words I need to hear will
G
D/F♯
C(add2)
al - ways get me through the day and make it o - kay.
D
C
Em
I miss you.
C
Em
C
Em
Dsus
D5
5fr
rit.

EVERYTHING BACK BUT YOU

Words and Music by AVRIL LAVIGNE
and BUTCH WALKER

Copyright © 2007 ALMO MUSIC CORP., AVRIL LAVIGNE PUBLISHING LTD., EMI BLACKWOOD MUSIC INC. and SONOTROCK MUSIC
All Rights for AVRIL LAVIGNE PUBLISHING LTD. Controlled and Administered by ALMO MUSIC CORP.
All Rights for SONOTROCK MUSIC Controlled and Administered by EMI BLACKWOOD MUSIC INC.
All Rights Reserved Used by Permission

F♯5
went through hell. I
all a - long that
A5
5fr
B5
wish I could re - move it from my mind.
you weren't the right one for me.
E5
My Two months a -
friends tried to
F♯5
way from you, but I could - n't
tell me to be

A5
5fr
tell; I thought that ev - 'ry - thing was gon - na be just
strong. I bet you did - n't think that I would
B5
fine.
see.
The
C♯m
4fr
post - card that you wrote with the stu - pid lit - tle
A
note, some - thing was - n't quite right a -
E

B
C♯m
4fr
bout it.
(1., 3.) It smelled like cheap per -
(2.) I wan - na see you
A
fume and it did - n't smell like you.
cry like I did a thou - sand times.
E
Bsus2
There is no way you can get a - round it,
Now you're los - ing me, you're los - ing me now
be -
B5
E
cause you wrote, "I wish you were

F♯7sus
her." You left out the
E/A
"e." You left with - out me, and
G♯5
4fr
A5
5fr
Bsus
E
now you're some - where out there with a hey, hey,
F♯7sus
psy - cho babe. I hate you. Why are guys so lame?

E/A
G♯5
4fr
To Coda
Ev - 'ry - thing I gave you, I want ev - 'ry - thing
A5
5fr
Bsus
1
E
back but you.
F♯7sus
E/A
G♯5
4fr
A5
5fr
Bsus
My

2
E
F♯5
you.
A5
5fr
G♯5
4fr
A5
5fr
B5
E
F♯5

A5
5fr
G♯5
4fr
A5
5fr
B5
D.S. al Coda
The
CODA
A5
5fr
Bsus
back
but
("I
E
F♯7sus
wish you were her."
you.
You left out the
"e."
You left with - out me.)
E/A

G♯5
4fr
1
A5
5fr
Bsus
2
A5
5fr
Bsus
Ev - 'ry - thing
back
but
("I
back
but
E
Esus
you.
E5

HOT

Words and Music by AVRIL LAVIGNE
and EVAN TAUBENFELD

Copyright © 2007 ALMO MUSIC CORP., AVRIL LAVIGNE PUBLISHING LTD., EMI APRIL MUSIC INC. and BIG EVIL MUSIC CO.
All Rights for AVRIL LAVIGNE PUBLISHING LTD. Controlled and Administered by ALMO MUSIC CORP.
All Rights for BIG EVIL MUSIC CO. Controlled and Administered by EMI APRIL MUSIC INC.
All Rights Reserved Used by Permission

A♭5
4fr
F5
I want to lock you up in my clos -
I can make you feel all bet -
C5
3fr
D♭5
4fr
A♭5
4fr
- et, where no one's a - round.
- ter, just take it in,
I want to
and I can
F5
C5
3fr
put your hand in my pock - et, be -
show you all the plac - es you've
D♭5
4fr
A♭
4fr
cause you're al - lowed.
nev - er been.
I want to
And I can

F5
C5
3fr
drive you in - to the cor - ner and
make you say ev - 'ry - thing that
D♭
A♭
4fr
kiss you with - out a sound. I want to
you've nev - er said. And I will
F5
C5
3fr
stay this way for - ev - er; I'll
let you do an - y - thing a -
D♭
B♭5
say it loud.
gain and a - gain.
Now you're in

D♭5
4fr
and you can't get out.
You make me so
E♭5
6fr
hot, make me wan - na
B♭5
drop. You're so ri - dic - u -
D♭5
4fr
lous I can bare - ly
A♭5
4fr
stop. I can hard - ly
E♭5
6fr
breathe; you make me wan - na
B♭5
scream. You're so fab - u -

D♭5
4fr
A♭5
4fr
lous. You're so good to me, ba - by,
E♭5
6fr
B♭sus
ba - by. You're
A♭/D♭
4fr
D♭sus2
4fr
A♭5
4fr
so good to me, ba - by,
E♭5
6fr
B♭7sus
ba - by.
1
D♭sus2
4fr

2
D♭sus2
4fr
B♭m
D♭
Kiss me gen - tly.
A♭
4fr
E♭(add4)
B♭m
al - ways, I know. Hold me,
D♭
A♭
4fr
E♭(add4)
love me, don't ev - er go,
B♭m
D♭
A♭
4fr
oh,

E♭(add4)
B♭m
D♭sus2
4fr
yeah.
A♭5
4fr
E♭5
6fr
You make me so hot, make me wan - na
B♭5
D♭5
4fr
A♭5
4fr
drop. You're so ri - dic - u - lous I can bare - ly stop. I can hard - ly
E♭5
6fr
B♭5
D♭5
4fr
breathe; you make me wan - na scream. You're so fab - u - lous. You're so good to

1
A♭5
4fr
2
A♭
4fr
E♭
3fr
me. You make me so me, ba - by, ba - by.
B♭sus
A♭/D♭
4fr
D♭sus2
4fr
A♭
4fr
You're so good to me, ba - by,
E♭
3fr
B♭7sus
D♭sus2
4fr
ba - by.
Optional Ending
Repeat and Fade

INNOCENCE

Words and Music by AVRIL LAVIGNE
and EVAN TAUBENFELD

Copyright © 2007 ALMO MUSIC CORP., AVRIL LAVIGNE PUBLISHING LTD., EMI APRIL MUSIC INC. and BIG EVIL MUSIC CO.
All Rights for AVRIL LAVIGNE PUBLISHING LTD. Controlled and Administered by ALMO MUSIC CORP.
All Rights for BIG EVIL MUSIC CO. Controlled and Administered by EMI APRIL MUSIC INC.
All Rights Reserved Used by Permission

Amaj7
C♯m
4fr
round and now I'm so a - mazed. I think a - bout the
long, I'm so hap - py here. It's so strong, and now I
Amaj7
B
lit - tle things that make life great.
let my - self be sin - cere.
I would - n't change a
Amaj7
B
thing a - bout it. This is the
A
B
best feel - ing.

C♯m
4fr
Amaj7
E
This in - no - cence is bril - liant. I
B
C♯m
4fr
Amaj7
hope that it will stay. This mo - ment is per - fect.
E
B
C♯m
4fr
Please don't go a - way; I need
A
E
B
you now, and I'll

Amaj7
1
B
B(add4)
hold on - to it. Don't you
B
C♯m
4fr
let it pass you by.
Amaj7
C♯m
4fr
Amaj7
2
B7
Amaj7
Don't you let it pass you by. It's a state of bliss; you

E
B
think you're dream - ing. It's the hap - pi - ness in -
C♯m
4fr
Amaj7
E
side that you're feel - ing. It's so beau - ti - ful, it makes you wan - na cry.
B
Amaj7
It's the state of bliss; you
E
B
think you're dream - ing. It's the hap - pi - ness in -

C♯m
4fr
Amaj7
side that you're feel - ing. It's so beau - ti - ful, it
E
B
makes you wan - na cry.
C♯m
4fr
(It's so beau - ti - ful, it makes you wan - na cry.)
This in - no - cence
Amaj7
E
B
is bril - liant.
(It makes me wan - na cry.

C♯m
4fr
Amaj7
E
This in - no - cence is bril - liant.
B
C♯m
4fr
A
Please don't go a - way, 'cause I need you now,
E
B
Amaj7
and I'll hold on -
B7
to it. Don't you let it pass you by.

C♯m
4fr
Amaj7
E
This in - no - cence is bril - liant.
I
B
C♯m
4fr
Amaj7
hope that it will stay. This mo - ment is per - fect.
E
B
C♯m
4fr
Please don't go a - way. I need
A
E
B
you now,
and I'll

Amaj7
B
hold on - to it. Don't you
C♯m
4fr
Amaj7
let it pass you by.
C♯m
4fr
Amaj7
C♯m
4fr
Amaj7
C♯m
4fr
Amaj9
rit.

I DON'T HAVE TO TRY

Words and Music by AVRIL LAVIGNE
and LUKASZ GOTTWALD

* *Recorded a half step lower.*

Copyright © 2007 ALMO MUSIC CORP., AVRIL LAVIGNE PUBLISHING LTD., KOBALT SONGS MUSIC PUBLISHING and KASZ MONEY PUBLISHING
All Rights for AVRIL LAVIGNE PUBLISHING LTD. Controlled and Administered by ALMO MUSIC CORP.
All Rights for KASZ MONEY PUBLISHING Controlled and Administered by KOBALT SONGS MUSIC PUBLISHING
All Rights Reserved Used by Permission

C
G7sus
I wear the pants.
Am
F6
A5
5fr
G5
3fr
C5
3fr
Hey you, fol - low me.
Don't you dis - a - gree,
G5
3fr
C5
3fr
I'll take the lead,
be-cause you know
can't you see?
it's all a - bout

D5
5fr
A5
5fr
me.
Don't you
Be at
G5
3fr
C5
3fr
ques - tion me;
my beck and call.
G5
3fr
C5
3fr
you just do
I'm a know - it - all
what I say.
and it's all your fault.
D5
5fr
A5
5fr
I don't care

G5
3fr
C5
3fr
what you're say - ing, I don't care
G5
3fr
what you're think - ing. I don't care a - bout
C5
3fr
D5
5fr
an - y - thing. Get read - y, get read - y, 'cause I'm hap - pen - ing.
A5
5fr
G5
3fr
C5
3fr
I don't care what you're say - ing, I don't care

G5
3fr
C5
3fr
what you're think - ing.
I don't care a - bout an - y - thing.
Get
D5
5fr
𝄋 C5
3fr
read - y, get read - y, 'cause I'm on the scene.
I don't
E5
A5
5fr
F5
have to try
to make
C5
3fr
E5
you re - al - ize,

A5
5fr
F5
C5
3fr
G5
3fr
an - y - thing I wan - na do, an - y - thing I'm gon - na do,
A5
5fr
F5
To Coda
an - y - thing I wan - na do, I do, and
C5
3fr
E5
A5
5fr
I don't have to try.

F5
C
G7sus
Am
F6
C
G7sus
Am
F6
A5
5fr
1
C5
3fr
2
G5
3fr
Am

B7sus
2fr
C6
Dsus2
Esus
Gsus2
A5
5fr
Am/B
C/B
D.S. al Coda
CODA
C5
3fr
I
don't have
E5
A5
5fr
Fmaj7(no3rd)
3fr
to try.
(Don't have to try.)

ONE OF THOSE GIRLS

Words and Music by AVRIL LAVIGNE
and EVAN TAUBENFELD

* *Recorded one step lower.*

Copyright © 2007 ALMO MUSIC CORP., AVRIL LAVIGNE PUBLISHING LTD., EMI APRIL MUSIC INC. and BIG EVIL MUSIC CO.
All Rights for AVRIL LAVIGNE PUBLISHING LTD. Controlled and Administered by ALMO MUSIC CORP.
All Rights for BIG EVIL MUSIC CO. Controlled and Administered by EMI APRIL MUSIC INC.
All Rights Reserved Used by Permission

A♭5
4fr
You on - ly care a - bout one thing:
at least that's what they say.
C5
3fr
who you've seen or where you've been,
It's been a while, you're in de - ni -
A♭5
4fr
who's got mon - ey.
- al, and now it's too late.
E♭5
6fr
I see that look in your eyes;
The way she looks, it makes you high.

A♭5
4fr
it tells a mil - lion lies,
All the warn - ing signs,
C5
3fr
but deep in - side I know why
'cause her blonde hair, her blue eyes,
A♭5
4fr
you're talk - ing to him.
it makes you wan - na die.
E♭/G
3fr
A♭5
4fr
I know what you're she's all a - bout; I

Adim
B♭sus
real - ly hope
he fig - ures
you fig - ure
it out.
She's
E♭5
6fr
F5
one of those girls,
noth - ing but trou - ble.
A♭5
4fr
Just one look and now you're see - ing dou - ble.
E♭5
6fr
F5
A♭5
4fr
Be - fore you know it she'll be gone,

C5
3fr
B♭5
E♭5
6fr
off to the next one. She's so good that
F5
A♭5
4fr
you won't see it com - ing; she'll take you for a ride and
E♭5
6fr
you'll be left with noth - ing. You'll be bro -
F5
A♭5
4fr
C5
3fr
B♭5
To Coda
- ken, she'll be gone, off to the next one.

1
E♭5
6fr
F5
A♭5
4fr
E♭5
6fr
F5
Off to the next one.
A♭5
4fr
2
Cm7
3fr
You know it's a game,
A♭sus2
3fr
you know it's a game.
She keeps

E♭
3fr
play - ing a - round with your head,
B♭
play - ing a - round with your head.
Cm7
3fr
She's so in - sane, so in - sane.
A♭sus2
3fr
She's the one to blame,
E♭
3fr

Bb
D.S. al Coda
she's the one to blame.
She's
CODA
Eb5
6fr
Ab5
4fr
Cm7
3fr
Ab5
4fr
Bb5
Eb5
6fr
Ab5
4fr
Off to the next one.
C5
3fr
B5/F#
Bb5/F
Eb5
6fr
Off to the next one.

CONTAGIOUS

Words and Music by AVRIL LAVIGNE
and EVAN TAUBENFELD

* *Recorded a half step lower.*

Copyright © 2007 ALMO MUSIC CORP., AVRIL LAVIGNE PUBLISHING LTD., EMI APRIL MUSIC INC. and BIG EVIL MUSIC CO.
All Rights for AVRIL LAVIGNE PUBLISHING LTD. Controlled and Administered by ALMO MUSIC CORP.
All Rights for BIG EVIL MUSIC CO. Controlled and Administered by EMI APRIL MUSIC INC.
All Rights Reserved Used by Permission

D
D/F♯
G5
3fr
talk to you.
an - y - thing;
I do not know what I should
I think I've got you fig - ured
D
D/F♯
G5
3fr
say, and
out. So
I walk out in si - lence.
That's
D5
5fr
A5
5fr
D/F♯
when I start to re - al - ize
what you bring to my
G5
3fr
D
life.
Damn, this guy can make me
cry -
smi -

A
D/G
D
- y - y.
- i - ile.
It's so con -
A
Bm
D/G
D
ta - gious.
I can - not get it out
A
Bm
D/G
D
A
Bm
of my mind. It's so out - ra - geous.
You
D/G
D
F♯7(no3rd)
4fr
make me feel so
high
high.

1
2
all the time.
G
D(add4)
3fr
G
I will give you ev - 'ry - thing.
I will treat you
D(add4)
3fr
G
D(add4)
3fr
right.
If you just
give me a chance,
F♯7(no3rd)
4fr
I can prove I'm right.
It's

D/G
D
A
Bm
D/G
D
so con - ta - gious. I can - not get it out
A
Bm
D/G
D
A
Bm
of my mind. It's so out - ra - geous. You
D/G
D
1
F♯7(no3rd)
4fr
make me feel so high.
It's
2
F♯7(no3rd)
4fr
high all the time.

KEEP HOLDING ON

from the Twentieth Century Fox Motion Picture ERAGON

Words and Music by AVRIL LAVIGNE
and LUKAS GOTTWALD

Copyright © 2006 T C F Music Publishing, Inc., Almo Music Corp., Avril Lavigne Publishing Ltd., Kobalt Songs Music Publishing and Kasz Money Publishing
All Rights for Avril Lavigne Publishing Ltd. Controlled and Administered by Almo Music Corp.
All Rights for Kasz Money Publishing Controlled and Administered by Kobalt Songs Music Publishing
All Rights Reserved Used by Permission

Em7
Csus2
Em7
in.
fend.
No, I won't give in.
I'll fight and de - fend.
Csus2
D7sus
G5
G5/F♯
Keep
hold - ing
Em7
Csus2
G5
on
'cause you know we'll make it through, we'll make it through.
Just
G5/F♯
Em7
Csus2
stay
strong
'cause you know I'm here for you, I'm here for you.

G5
3fr
G5/F♯
Em7
There's noth-ing you can say, noth-ing you can do. There's no oth-er way when it comes
Csus2
3fr
G5
3fr
G5/F♯
to the truth so keep hold - ing
Em7
Csus2
3fr
To Coda
Am
on 'cause you know we'll make it through, we'll make it through. Hear me when I say, when I say
C
Am
Em
I be - lieve that noth-in's gon - na change, noth-in's gon - na change des - ti - ny.

Am
C
What-ev-er's meant to be will work out per-fect-ly, yeah, yeah,
D
G5
3fr
G5/F♯
yeah, yeah. La, da, da, da, la, da, da, da,
Em7
Csus2
3fr
D.S. al Coda
la, da, da, da, da, da, da.
CODA
G5
3fr
G5/F♯
Em7
Csus2
3fr
Keep hold-ing on.

G5
3fr
G5/F♯
Em7
Keep
Csus2
3fr
G5
3fr
G5/F♯
hold - ing on.
There's noth-in' you can say,
noth-in' you can do.
Em7
Csus2
3fr
G5
3fr
There's no oth - er way when it comes to the truth so keep
G5/F♯
Em7
Csus2
3fr
hold - ing on 'cause you know we'll make it through, we'll make it through.